SELF DISCOVERY JOURNAL

121 Thought Provoking Questions

Journal Questions for Women

(Notebook)

By

Shalu Sharma

http://www.shalusharma.net
info@ShaluSharma.com
www.amazon.com/author/shalusharma

This journal belongs to:

Table of contents

Writing to clear your mind

We all go through life trying to figure out who we are and where we fit into this crazy world. It takes some people their entire lives before they finally figure it out. For others, they figure it out early on and then excel in their passion throughout the rest of their lives. There is really no way of knowing at what point in your life you will be able to figure everything out. However, this doesn't mean you have to wait around for a miracle to happen either. Instead, you should write your thoughts inside a diary to clear your mind and let the answers come to you.

People tend to get confused in their lives because they have all of these thoughts racing through them, but they don't know how to organize them all. So they keep going back and forth in their minds about doing one thing versus doing another thing. In the end, they do nothing because they keep thinking instead of doing. Writing down your thoughts is a way to have the best of both worlds. It allows you to be a doer by writing down your thoughts and sorting them out for you to see on paper. Sometimes it helps to see your thoughts organized and written out. That way you can study and make sense of them all. Otherwise, you will continue to go back and forth in your mind over the thoughts you previously had, but have now forgotten. Writing takes the pressure off of having to remember your thoughts.

The great thing about keeping a diary is there are no rules. You can write whatever you want inside a diary and it will be yours to view only. It is almost like expressing yourself to a therapist, but instead of talking to a person you are writing in a book. A diary is a book of discrete literature that describes the personal events or encounters that the author experienced. Diaries are not meant to be seen by anyone else except for the author. It is a way for them to sort out their feelings and emotions without having to pay a lot of money to go see a psychiatrist. Diaries are often referred to as journals or records of someone's life because the person documents every major event that happened to them. It also documents every secret feeling or thought they have as well. For teenagers, their diaries will contain their secret crushes at school or the people they don't like the most. As for adults, their diary entries are about their current state of happiness and the changes they want to make in their lives. These entries will likely talk about their spouse, partner, job and overall situation in life. But no matter what your age or social status is in this world, keeping a journal that lets you expresses your innermost feelings is a way of finding peace of mind and happiness. That is the most important reason for keeping a diary in the first place. In this book there are 121 questions for you to write and release the stress of daily life.

Benefits of writing a diary and regular journaling

There are many benefits to writing a diary. One of the biggest benefits is self discovery. Often times we get so caught up with the chaos of everyday life that we don't stop and think about our position in this world. We tend to just accept other people's interpretation of who we are instead of trying to determine that for ourselves. How often have you just sat down and started thinking about your life and what you want out of it? Most people live such hectic lifestyles that they never give themselves a chance to answer this question. Writing a diary will allow you to sort out your feelings and determine what you want to accomplish in this world before your life is over. As you continuously write in your diary and think about your life, you may discover new wants and desires that you never had the courage to admit to yourself before. Then you can finally know who you are and get clarification on all the thoughts and feelings that you possess.

Diaries of journals can be a form of therapy for the author. Have you ever noticed how it hurts to keep your feelings and thoughts bottled up inside of you? Some people choose to go to a psychiatrist to express their feelings, while others may not want to tell another person their private thoughts. But they still want to get their thoughts and feelings out of their system, so they can feel better. A diary is a great alternative because you can still remain discrete with your feelings and let them out of your system at the same time. Writing your personal thoughts in a diary can feel just as relieving as telling another person. Not only that, but it will help reduce your stress and anxiety levels as well. As you probably know, stress can be bad for your physical and mental health. Many people have heart attacks and strokes because of their high levels of stress. Writing in a diary could actually help you maintain your physical health by reducing your stress and living a happier life with peace of mind.

Believe it or not, writing in a diary can actually make you smarter because it enhances your cognitive function by allowing you to think more. In this day and age, people like to actually avoid thinking whenever they can. Have you ever noticed how people are constantly listening to earphones or watching movies on their smart-phones when they have nothing else to do? These kinds of activities prevent people from thinking and just let them be in a state of sedation. On the other hand, writing in a diary lets people think deeply about themselves and what they want to accomplish. This will exercise their brain and allow them to be better thinkers in future. At the same time, they will have a list of thoughts written down that will outline their goals for the future. Then they can use this list as a way to work towards their goals by frequently referring back to them.

How to keep a diary?

A traditional diary comes in the form of a physical book or journal. For many hundreds of years, people wrote inside physical diaries with a pen or pencil. The technology behind it is simple because you can turn any kind of blank book into a diary. If you go to an office supply store you can find all kinds of notebooks and composition books that have cardboard covers and blank sheets of paper inside of them. Each notebook costs less than $1 on average. If you wanted to start a diary in this fashion then you could just purchase one of these books and then buy a set of pens for $2. This would be everything you would need to start your own diary. Then as you continue to fill up the notebooks with your entries, you can purchase more books or maybe even bigger books that have more pages in them. Just make sure you don't lose track of all the books if you have to use multiple ones. In this book, there are a series of questions that you attempt to write and keep everything in one place.

Another way to keep a diary is to take advantage of modern technology and use a diary app. If you were to search the Apple or Google Play stores, you can find dozens of diary apps. The great thing about them is they are easier to secure than physical diaries. Diary apps generally have password protection of the entries. That way if some random person finds your phone then they wouldn't be able to read your entries. You can't get this kind of security with a physical diary because anyone can open those up and see what's inside. Plus, you can create thousands of pages with your diary apps. The amount of pages is basically determined by the amount of memory you have on your phone. But since diary pages use very little memory, you could literally write every thought you ever had in a diary app and still never run out of memory. Therefore, you diary preference should depend on the level of security and convenience you would prefer. Some people find it easier to use the virtual keyboards on their tablets or smart phones, whereas others prefer physically writing with their pen. Either choice is fine.

This book contains all the questions you need. All you need is a pen and some space and time. You don't have to spend a lot of time writing in it. Just spend a few minutes per day devoted to your journal. Each entry will simply contain the most important thoughts and feelings for that particular question. You aren't writing a book of thoughts that will be 100 pages long in a single day. Your diary entries should only contain the current thoughts you have on the day you write it. This means you will be writing few pages at the most. However, there are some exceptions to the rule. If you haven't written in your diary for a long period of time then you might want to catch up and write about what's happened to you since your last entry. Of course, this will take much longer than 20 minutes if you do it this way. But for time management purposes, it is best to just devote a small portion of time per day to creating an entry.

The questions

Describe yourself in five words or sentences?

What are the things that make you happy?

What worries you the most?

If you had lots of money what would you do?

Who do you love the most?

Who's the important person in the world?

If you lost everything, what would you do and where would you go?

Would you like to be immortal?

What do you think of sex?

Which part of your body you like being touched?

How is your relationship with you parents?

What do you like the most and hate the most about your parents?

If you had a chance, would you change your partner for another one?

What do you like the most and hate about your partner?

Do you like your job?

What's your dream job?

What do you like to wear and why?

Do you believe in God?

On judgement day, if God asked you why he would let you in heaven, what would you say?

What makes you smile?

Have you hurt anyone?

Do you hate anyone?

What is the most outrageous thing you have ever done?

What are you scared of?

What is one thing that matters to you the most and why?

Have you done anything lately to make someone smile?

How long do you want to live?

Have you ever broken the law?

What is worse: never trying or trying but failing many times?

What is the worst thing that has ever happened to you?

What is the worst thing you have ever done?

What is the best thing that has ever happened to you?

Are you happy with your body?

What would you change about your body?

What would you change about your personality?

Do people like you?

What do you think your life would be like 10 years from now?

Which one of your friends would you like me to meet?

Who are your best friends and would they help you out if you needed them?

What kind of people do you like?

What would you do if you were famous?

Have you ever given charity? Why or why not?

If you were to be reborn again, what would you like to reborn as?

Is there one thing that you want most out of life?

How would you like to be remembered?

If you were to get cancer and had one year to live, what would you do and how would you live your life?

What is your worst nightmare?

How would you like to die?

What does success actually mean to you?

How do you spend your free time?

One place that you would like to travel to and why?

Which bad habits you would like to get rid off?

Take yourself ten years back! What would you like to change about your life?

What are your goals in life?

How do you plan to achieve them?

What do you want the most in life?

What inspires you the most?

Is there something that no one knows about you other than yourself?

If you had to make one minute speech to the world, what would you say?

So far in life, what do you regret the most?

What are you most proud of?

Are you afraid of dying?

Can you spend 2 days alone on an island?

Do you gossip?

What are you tolerating?

What matters most in your career?

What is your ideal self?

Are you living the life of your dreams?

Do you have a dream that you would like to be fulfilled?

What are the top priorities of your life right now?

What is your favourite food?

What good habits you would have liked to have?

What TV programmes you like watching the most and why?

Are you jealous of anyone and why?

How do you express your anger?

Are you a good person?

If I were to spend a day with you, what will you do with me?

If you had three wishes, what would those wishes be?

Do you think the more money you would have the happier you would be?

If money was no issue, where would you live and why?

What is your favourite song and why do you like it?

Who do you admire the most and why?

What is the biggest lie you have told?

Is there anything you feel guilty about?

What is your biggest desire?

Do you have a sexual fantasy?

Can you go topless on the beach?

What was the most terrifying moment of your life and why?

What are the things that you can’t go without?

What are your safest memories?

What are the things you did with your mum when you were little?

If you could go back in time, what are the things you would change?

Do you have a favourite book that you read again and again?

What is the biggest mistake of your life?

What is the mistake you never want to make?

Write a letter to your favourite actor or actress.

Write about your first crush.

How do like to sleep at night?

What is your most valuable possession and what would you do if you lost it?

What was your new year's resolution this year and what will it be next year?

What are the things that make you safe?

What makes you laugh?

If you could fly where would you go and why?

What are your top achievements?

Do you procrastinate about anything?

If you had a magic wand what would you change in an instance?

What are your weaknesses?

If you vote in the next election, who would you vote for and why?

What are the things you can say yes to?

What are the things you can say no to?

When do you feel most energized?

Describe your favourite season and why you like it?

If you had magic powers, what would that be?

How do you see your life when you are older?

What is your ideal outfit?

What is the best surprise you ever had in your life?

What is the meaning of life in your opinion?

What are the things you really want right now?

What are the things that stress you out?

What are your earliest memories?

Are there things that remind you of your childhood? Describe it.

50816273R00075

Made in the USA
Middletown, DE
27 June 2019